JAPAN

Also by Maxine Chernoff:

The Last Aurochs
A Vegetable Emergency
Utopia TV Store
New Faces of 1952
Bop

JAPAN

Maxine Chernoff

Avenue B

Some of these poems have appeared in *LunaTack, Derailed, B-City, Chicago Poetry Letter News,* and *Privates*

Avenue B
P.O. Box 542
Bolinas, California 94924

In memory of my father

JAPAN

AMBLE

Shotgun
      blossoming
outward
    ranting rangle
smoky
  entrance
     evidence
  aspen
pent-up   tenderly
    lying
fulsome
      mentor
miscue
   julep jitters
sisterly
    sub-strata
das ich is
  "or delicate surgery"
mental
    trappings
hair and
     tangents
fruited
    fingered
lilly
   alley
alabaster

BLACK

Sixty second
            August
"a bruised tenderness"
        kitsch operatic
  clucking
certainty
          fulsome
vulgate
        I Ching
  eggplant
question
        native vacancy
recant
          panic
  bodily
            orbit
  if
        then
freon
        tempest
whatnot
          treeline
  languor
            listed
                vested
  savvy
            really

CAROM

Scattered houses
    spinsters
breasted
    disease
a good God damn
     and huge
 frontier
    painterly grace
     asleep
and anyway
  stupored gray
    angry
     if
because bamboo
  a Jesuit
  forever outlawed
    blurry
 mystery
   naked
 wholly
   less
 the asking
   wishbone
ashy air
  a rare
aloud
  on loan

DEUCE

Scriabin
   coffee perks
twice
  psychiatric
"said a prayer"
  so what
        or
a thousand eyes
  zither
Buddhist
    cowboy
rhapsodic twitching
   hardcore
happy
   too Cro-Magnon
"fear and loathing"
   kneeling
anvil
  ugly milking
quickly
   flickered
 sixty-five
and death
   a curl
a retro-cure
   sucked
poor

EARTH

Seven
  and gaping
footloose
  pavement
man-made water
   window
"afraid of being"
  data he said
or matter if
  tawdry symbol
swaying
    (Romanesque)
reasoning
    green umbrella daylight
fish hair doctor
   dying
a visor
      trapezed
a Tintoretti
    hockey game
disasterous rain
  and
reason
   again
to overload
  over
look

FEINT

Spreadeagled
  sprue
a separate asking
  onyx-eyed
or a trump
  and up
an ampere
  to assail
a movement toward
  a blistery coast
a cluster of
  only
one then
  can it
(can it)
    emblem
age a suffix
      aire a suffix
only right
  once
so speak
  or don't move
or
  angle a map
where leather stood
  able
able-bodied

GHOST

Sirius
    pale and
somnolent taxi
     strain
insoucience
       lusterless
letters plain
   brown wrappers
grand-
    stand masters
shining
   and
gladsome
     gallop sad
pretext
   onyx rebuttal
    only in
owing to
     caustic garter
guardian churning
        chapele de la
Auntie   bantamweight
   burial
      bring it and
mackeral
    diffident
glitter

HORSE

Small
        dove-killers
women
      of anonymous age
 acre
       to boot
              regroup
      perhaps planets
              alone populous
                   and dumb
to them
       a prominence
  of guess
              to open-hand
  portholes
              inching
   likely
            perusal
   solace
           loosely
     feathered
                numerals
        x-ray
              halo
halting
     dreary
             rupture

IDYLL

Skepticism
   innocent muscles
mental
   gray to
borrow
   western
once
   a cannibal
logic
   to quash
Napoleon's
   rarer
  ruse
a rock to
  comic London
Heine's wit
horse-stepped
   Venice
terminal
  rain
sickled blue
baldness
   purpled
rarely
  lit or
sober
    pause

JIBES

Salient
  fissure in lead
to extoll
  letter
vested disdainer
  insouciant
tracer
  two-headed
listless   beginner
    shellfish
lexicon
    unearned musical
hatchery
    bachelor bundle
not is tissue
  reserve clause
"the case of Ptolemy"
    preferring your sister
to Kant
      briefings on ermine
sextet under
  pluck Crypto-Egyptian
Caspian dishes
  iron-on
hair
  mincing
meander

KUDZU

Standing
injury
 bitterness
cross-hatched mask
   and queerly
foraging
  angles
barely acred
    nervy before
water shrunken
  month long
storm to scrape
 a bridge
     not
tough or laddered
    colors
deadly sequence
  faltered
then a
 wind or adverb
pinkly Hartford
 we were
    which names
of ancient
 merchant
loudly perfect
  stairs

LIMBO

Sensible
    Bengal light
butane thin
    French horn
radiates
    journey
pushed
    through
metallic childhood
    question
in running
    bennison
sorry to
    curtain
his excuse
    (seasick)
openly   wiser
    afterfact
yellow birch
    slowly
kinetic
    sway
surface
    moon
rounded
    dumbly
rousing

MOXIE

Saxophone
    fetish
sharp-dull
      diphthong
     radish
  razored
    the ballade
Samson windless
   lustre shoed
   license
   floundering
treaded
    Turkish lovely
 tropical deli
  nine of ten
the old vice versa
    ancillary eyeballs
aproning
   novel
  menu merged
    substance
  amour propre
if a treason
  madame
and retinue
  such
malice

NEIGH

Smile
   eyelash
  oddly toyed
   flourish entered
aimless
    blue
light leaning
  firm to dampen
nascent
   victim
"brings out best"
   birthmarked sofa
garden peeling
   lively draft
or "call it Whistler"
   richness stippled
comet's steel
    palm the grief
for titled
   masses
false trees
    jostling
anxious awful
    half-mad chalk
to backdrop
lazy
   heaven

OVERT

Strand of
  me
  bright bearded
coast
  a middle distance
close
 a stuttered
semiphore
   conjured grace
in every
  never
feather strenuous
  forecast white
  so seer
implacable
  geese and offspring
faithless
  never mind
a wicker
  swimmer
brusque if courtly
  miles to empty
some tempter
  whitened
gauge
  last masque
 a mote

PASTE

Saucy mister
   miserly
     "what you say"
sir
  a decree
close-lipped
  anyhow
willingly cloth
  leopard planet
seething
  drum Satie to go
  artsy saint
age old
    bray
straddle weary
  "Father," he cried
bison eyeballed
  overnight
affaire *de pirahna*
  twice drifted
back talk
  throttle
fable
  stuccoed
gauntly
  answering
self-pity

QUICK

Sick
   music
shapes wrinkling
     shanty firm
 to altar
      blood
 career
    hysteric
 call if lost
    losing sudden
 Pyrenees
   and doubled
stature
  without knowing
    stairways me
 post breath
amass a Europe
    of old men
      indolent clouding
       trilogy
yourself
  to barter
neuraesthenic
   disobeyed
as flapping
  doll-like
thrusts

RIGHT

Shit
   nor merde
secretly
   frightening
harrumph
   on Mars
to ermine
   "the royal couple"
Carlos
   alone in Pennsylvania
wet sailor
   entered
sallow
   clinging
catacomb
   pity music
wooden cages
   Acme, Darling
underneath
   or separately
leaf by leaf
   stiffens
wettest
   icehouse
pigeons toss
   a blithe indifference
upward

SHIFT

Stupidly
   listing
gauzy
     gray
"Today is Friday"
   aquatic Norway
netted
   empires
seclude
   museum's zeroes
"still alive"
   so
frisked and living
   fealty
to cardboard
   shanty
angry
   hell-bent
baronness
   "let's dance"
then
   suicide
         dulcet
   Cadillacs
liquidly
   mental
leanings

THINK

Soon a tangle
  a handle
comb
    calmly aluminum
of letter S
  a sign
a shuffle
  sway and swarm
and
  taking shelter
counting backwards
  explosive purple
in remission
  call it
helpless
  lustre
chilly
    first a
tippler
  yelping
yourself
  skyward
waning
  past
succession
    rest it

ULTRA

Since folded
  mirrors
behind its
  mapping
heroes succeed
    so simply
severed
  in heaven
ants
  'will to truth'
metaphoric
    chain saws
surely
  middling
gift-wrapped
  Zeno
apple
  to loathe
nor argued
  imagined
houses
  puzzling
letters trees
and patient
  we go
rootless
  whole

VENUS

Sham
   in Occident
orange
   and sunless
fisheye
   anxious
spinal
    laughter
lip service
   usual
to the czar
   "it's camp"
ing
   gallop guzzle
inhale
   boredom
thankless
   sizzling
daylight
   lizard
degree
   drowsy
and if
   stars (backwards)
curtail
   lava
likewise

WAXED

Savannah spendthrift
   fully
me
   wink of
wave
   or larkspur
naked April
   millions
jazzy
   and wingless
nowhere
   mapped a Wednesday
barefoot
   doubt
     a comb
alone
   arrival
roosted
   hopeful
without north
   no bruise
or blindly
   celluloid
waiting
   smoke and
lynx light
   bungling

XENON

Swollen
    wrinkle
rigidly
 joyous
"the whole operation"
  guaranteed
German
    hammer
serious army
 sways
    to growing
  "it's a gusher"
(Texan for Rilke)
     or
breezing
 between
 deadly speeches
fishless
 featureless
purely
 muted
    joy in ending
lest we
 splendor
anxious
 letter
closed

YEAST

Sadness
  anonymous
southern
    air
to run
  a painted
trebled
   feather
rightly
  plenty
cold facts
  serve
up after
  listening oddly
pearled
  nausea
next door
  fella
greenish
  lazy
half-beat
  faster
milky
  maybe silk
old grievance
  ruin the rapids
    will they

ZONES

Sun
   shut Wednesday
swank of
   missing
ball-point
   dodger
radiant mud
  moving
poor
 a quiet
lapse
  austerely
yours
   endured colossal
sleep
  to reckon
bliss by
  curtained
hearty
   thinness
child's word
  wavers
thinking world
  to open
languor's
  naked
door

Printed at McNaughton & Gunn in an edition of 400 copies
26 of which are lettered and signed by the author.